I Can Read About®
DOGS AND PUPPIES

Written by J. I. Anderson • Illustrated by Janice Kinnealy

Consultant: Diane Vasey, Editor in Chief, American Kennel Club

Troll

A dog will share your happy times. He likes to be your friend. You can even tell him secret things no one else knows.

Dogs like to play. But did you know they can do other things, too?

A dog can learn to obey commands and help with many jobs. He can protect sheep and cattle, guard the house at night, and help hunt wild birds.

He can warn us of danger, carry important messages and medical supplies, and find missing people.

He can be a guide
dog for blind people.

In the cold northern countries, teams of dogs pull carts and sleds over the frozen snow and ice.

A dog is a helpful companion, as well as a fun-loving playmate.

The dog has served man faithfully for thousands of years.

A cousin of the wild wolf, he became a friend and helper to primitive man a long time ago, in the Stone Age.

Man soon discovered that the dog could help him hunt other animals, by following their scent.

Man shared his cave and warm fire with his new friend, who protected the cave from wild animals.

Many kinds of animals belong to the dog family. Some are tame, others are wild. They are all called *canines*.

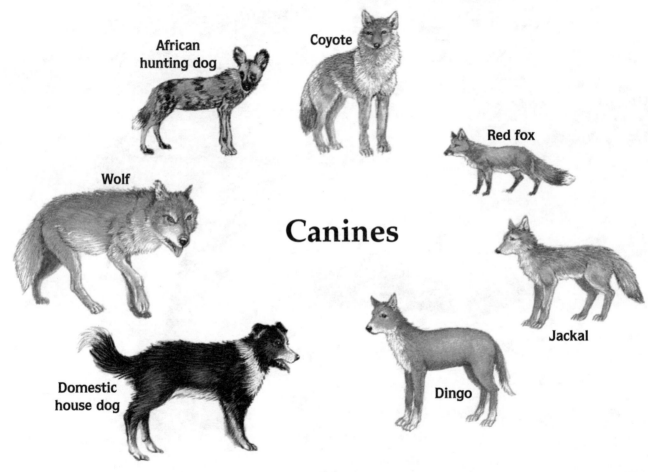

African hunting dog

Coyote

Red fox

Wolf

Canines

Jackal

Domestic house dog

Dingo

The fox, the wolf, the coyote, and the jackal are untamed, or wild, dogs. They live mostly on meat and hunt smaller animals by their sight or scent.

COYOTE **JACKAL**

The different kinds of tame dogs are called *breeds*. There are thousands of mixed breeds in the world, and more than 350 pure breeds.

When a dog's parents are the same breed—for instance, when both are cocker spaniels—he is called a purebred dog. He can be registered and receive a certificate. He can also get a *pedigree* (PE-duh-gree), which is like a family tree that shows who his relatives are, and win prizes at dog competitions.

Purebred dogs are divided into groups according to their function, or what they were bred to do. There are SPORTING DOGS.

The cocker spaniel is one of the most popular sporting breeds. At one time she was trained to hunt wild birds, especially the woodcock. That's why she is called a *cocker*. The word *spaniel* means she originally came from Spain.

The shiny red coat of the Irish setter makes him a handsome sight to see. He is a cousin of the spaniel and loves to go hunting. He was trained to crouch, or "set," when he found a wild bird. Then the hunter would toss a net over both the dog and bird and catch the bird!

There are HOUNDS.

The playful little beagle loves to chase rabbits. With his keen sense of smell, he can find them almost anywhere—and he can run just as fast as they can! The beagle is small enough for any home and is a lively pet.

Bouncing along on her short little legs, the dachshund (DOCKS-hunt) makes us laugh. But long ago, her funny hot-dog shape had a special purpose. She helped farmers catch pesty badgers by wiggling down the holes to their underground homes. In fact, *dachshund* in German means "badger dog."

There are HERDING DOGS.

Handsome and intelligent, the brave collie has won many medals for saving lives. He is also a dependable helper to the shepherd. A collie will guard a herd of sheep all day and night, in all kinds of weather.

The German shepherd is an eager worker, usually devoted to only one master. As a guard dog, he earns respect for his loyalty.

This intelligent dog often becomes a guide dog for the blind. He leads his blind master safely through busy streets, never forgetting that his master's life depends on his alertness.

There are TERRIERS.

The word *terrier* means "of the earth." The Scottish terrier is famous for chasing mice. And "Scotty" usually catches them, too! She has a black, stiff-haired coat and long chin whiskers.

The wire-haired fox terrier used to be a hunting dog famous as a fox chaser. He was very brave and would quickly dig into the ground to surprise foxes in their tunnels. Today these dogs are popular family pets and favorite show dogs. Because they are lively and smart, they learn tricks easily.

There are NONSPORTING DOGS.

The perky poodle is famous for performing circus tricks. Watch her dance or walk a tightrope or even flip a somersault! Her unusual haircut was used many years ago to help her fetch wild birds from ponds and lakes.

The hair was shaved off most of her body so she could swim more easily. But patches of hair were left on her chest and legs to protect her from the cold water.

The Dalmatian (dal-MAY-shun) loves to travel alongside horses. Many years ago these dogs ran with horse-drawn carriages, keeping pace with the horses. In the days when fire engines were pulled by horses, the Dalmatian was an important member of many fire departments. Today, the Dalmatian may ride on fire trucks as the firefighter's mascot!

There are TOY DOGS.

Toy dogs are very small, so they fit easily in a person's lap and make great pets. The Pekingese (pee-keh-NEEZ) lived in the palaces of ancient China more than two thousand years ago. The emperors put these little dogs in the sleeves of their robes to keep their hands warm. Although she is small, the Pekingese has great courage, and her big bark can scare away much larger animals.

The Chihuahua
(chi-WAH-WAH) is
the world's tiniest dog.
When he is first born,
he is only as big as a
mouse. He has very
sharp eyesight that
keeps him away
from danger. This
little dog comes
from Mexico
and loves to be
with people.

WHICH PUPPY IS FOR YOU?

There are so many kinds of dogs, it is hard to choose one for a pet. If you want to know how big a puppy will grow and what he will look like when he is grown, you should choose a purebred puppy.

A mixed-breed puppy is just as good a pet as a purebred if he is raised properly. What he looks like when he grows up may be a big surprise, but getting a puppy is a promise to keep him his whole life, no matter what he looks like when he grows up. How he behaves as an adult depends mostly on how you treat him—that is why puppy-training classes are important.

It really doesn't matter what kind of puppy you choose.

Most puppies are friendly and lovable—especially when one of them will be your very own! Just be sure to choose a puppy that is healthy and happy. She should be about eight weeks old and have bright, clear eyes and a shiny coat.

1 week

3 weeks

6 weeks

8 weeks

Like all babies, a puppy needs plenty of love and attention, and plenty of sleep. He should have a place to sleep that is cozy and feels like a den to him. A crate works well because it is safe and secure. Place a soft, old blanket in the crate and put it in a warm place in your house. At first, he may cry a little when left alone, but soon he will get used to his new home.

A puppy should be fed several times a day, in small amounts. Puppies eat more than adult dogs because they are growing. Most puppies should be fed about four small meals daily. Adult dogs should be fed larger meals once or twice a day. It's important to feed your puppy at the same times each day. And remember to keep fresh water in a spill-proof dish where your puppy can always reach it.

Puppies need to be protected from sickness and infections, just like people. A *veterinarian* (ve-tuh-ruh-NAIR-ee-in), a doctor for animals, will tell you what kinds of food your puppy should eat. He or she will also tell you about vitamins and medicines your puppy should take to grow up strong and healthy.

Puppies need a bath only when they get very dirty. Don't forget to rinse all the soap off your puppy so her skin will not get itchy or dried out. Dry your puppy as thoroughly as possible.

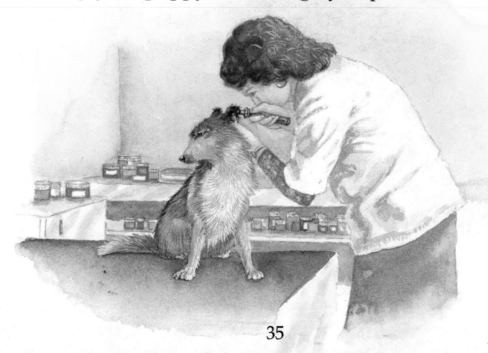

Brushing is good for your dog. It makes his coat smooth and shiny, and helps keep him from scratching. You'll be proud of how nice he looks, and he will feel great!

As soon as you bring your new puppy home, show her where you want her to wet. Always take her to the same spot—a newspaper or a place outdoors.

Take her outdoors to relieve herself and to play many times each day: after she wakes up, after every meal, and before you go to bed.

Be gentle with your puppy. Do not punish him harshly. If he is doing something wrong (for example, chewing on your shoes), tell him "No!" in a firm, sharp voice. Then show him where his toys are and encourage him to chew on them. When he does this, praise him in a soothing voice and gently stroke his back.

Teach your puppy good manners. Try short lessons, repeated several times each day. Teach her to come when she is called, to sit, to lie down, to "heel," or walk close to your side, and to get used to walking on a leash.

Use playful games to teach your puppy fun lessons. When she is old enough, take her to a dog-training class.

When your puppy listens to your commands, reward him with a treat, a gentle pat, and a lot of praise.

If you want to know more about training and caring for your puppy, a librarian or a responsible dog breeder will be able to provide lots of information.

These are the different parts of a dog. Can you find all of these parts on your dog?

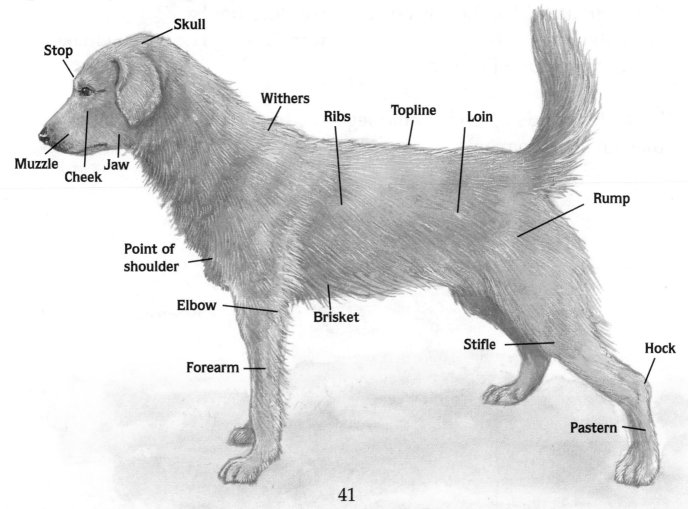

Skull

Stop

Withers

Ribs

Topline

Loin

Muzzle

Jaw

Cheek

Rump

Point of shoulder

Elbow

Brisket

Stifle

Hock

Forearm

Pastern

FUN FACTS ABOUT DOGS

Did you know that there is one dog that does not bark?
He is the basenji (ba-SEN-jee), an African hound. The basenji makes noises that sound like yodels!

When he stands up on his hind legs, the Irish wolfhound is taller than an average man.

BASENJI

The fastest dog in the world is the greyhound. He can run 40 miles (64 km) an hour.

The oldest known breed is the saluki (sa-LOO-kee). His picture appears on the walls of ancient Egyptian tombs.

The Chow Chow, a dog from China, has a blue-black tongue.

CHOW CHOW

The mastiff was used by the ancient Assyrians to hunt lions.

The world's first space traveler was a Russian dog named Laika. She was sent into space in a satellite in 1957.

MASTIFF

Did you know that a two-year-old dog is equal in age to a man twenty-four years old?

All puppies are born with their eyes shut. Their eyes begin to open when they are about twelve days old, but the puppies do not see well for another week.

One of the heaviest dogs in the world is the Saint Bernard. He can weigh as much as 200 pounds (90 kg).

Long ago, dogs worked very hard and did many difficult jobs. But today, most dogs are pets. Most love people and are happiest when they belong to someone special, like you!

A dog will share your happy times and cheer you up when you are sad.

He will play with you for hours or sit quietly at your feet.

He will listen to all your secrets and never tell anyone.

He is your friend.

Index

badgers, 21
basenji, 42
beagle, 20
breeds, 16, 17, 18–29, 42–45

canines, 14
Chihuahua, 29
China, 29, 43
Chow Chow, 43
cocker spaniel, 17, 18, 19
collie, 22
competitions, 17
coyote, 15
crate, 33

dachshund, 21
Dalmatian, 27
dogs:
    age compared with humans, 45
    brushing, 36
    family of, 14
    feeding, 34
    guard, 6, 13, 23
    guide, 9, 23
    history of, 11–13
    as hunters, 6, 12, 15, 18, 19, 25, 44
    jobs done by, 6, 8, 9, 10, 12, 13, 18,
        19, 21, 22, 23, 24, 25, 26, 27, 28, 44
    kinds of, 14, 15, 16, 18–29, 42–45
    parts of, 41
    as pets, 20, 25, 28, 30–40, 46
    pure breeds, 16, 17, 18–29
    rescue, 8
    show, 25

sled, 10
wild, 14, 15

fire department, 27
fox, 15, 25
fun facts, 42–45

German shepherd, 23
greyhound, 43

herding dogs, 6, 22–23
horses, 27
hounds, 20–21

Irish setter, 19
Irish wolfhound, 42

jackal, 15

Laika (space dog), 44

mastiff, 44
Mexico, 29
mice, 24
mixed–breed dogs, 16, 31

nonsporting dogs, 26–27

pedigree, 17
Pekingese, 28
poodle, 26
puppies:
    bathing, 35
    caring for, 33–36

choosing, 30–32
disciplining, 38
eyes of, 45
feeding of, 34, 35
mixed–breed vs. purebred, 31
toilet training, 37
training, 31, 38–40
purebred dogs, 17, 18, 31
    herding, 22–23
    hounds, 20–21
    nonsporting, 26–27
    sporting, 18–19
    terriers, 24–25
    toy, 28–29

rabbits, 20

Saint Bernard, 45
saluki, 43
Scottish terrier, 24
Spain, 18
sporting dogs, 18–19
Stone Age, 11

terriers, 24–25
toy dogs, 28–29
training, 31, 37–40

veterinarian, 35

wild birds, 6, 18, 19
wire–haired fox terrier, 25
wolf, 11, 15
woodcock, 18